Ah, the future. It w   ty.
Leisure for all. Perfe   ex
at the press of a bu   ut
to be climate breaka...   ss-
ness and genocide. We've crumbling schools and creaking
hospitals, job insecurity and a disintegrating transport
system. Politicians no longer bother to hide their cor-
ruption, and a supine media fails to hold them to account.
Cyberspace is increasingly taken over by shameless
grifters, by trolls and their culture wars, by a relentless
stoking up of anger. And the news is an unending
horrorshow.

And yet, and yet, and yet….

Amid all this, away from the make-believe of TV and
dead-eyed corporate lobbyists, people carry on doing
remarkable things. In here you'll find poems which cel-
ebrate unexpected moments of beauty and joy, and
revel in our common humanity. There are reflections and
re-imaginings. Small everyday resistances. Poems in praise
of the promise of sunrise.

Look after yourselves and each other, wherever you are.
Times are dark. Remember to sing.

Steve

And yes, in the dark times
we will sing
our voices fragile, unbroken
make the heavens ring

.

snapshots from the fall of home

Steve Pottinger

ISBN: 978-1-7394509-1-5

typeset by Steve at Ignite.
www.ignitebooks.co.uk

Printed and bound in the UK
by Bell & Bain Ltd,
Glasgow.

for you, and the song in your heart

Contents

many of the poems in this collection
have previously been published in anthologies,
or online

This photo with friends
was published in Setumag in Autumn 2023

The polski sklep has closed its doors
was shortlisted in the McLellan poetry comp 2021

The sun is shining at last, and
was published in Setumag in Autumn 2023

Crown & Sceptre...
Corodividednation
both feature in the CultureMatters anthology
'Dungheap Cockerel'

On living with a larger, expansionist neighbour
was published online by CultureMatters,
Poets' Republic, and Morning Star

Old man in The Scotia
was published by Prole

For George
was published online by CultureMatters
and features in the 'Black Lives Matter' anthology

7.19 in the evening...
came joint 2nd in the Poets & Players comp 2023

In a moment's pause
And this...
Fatima
all published online by CultureMattes

El Vaquita
was shortlisted in the Verve poetry comp 2023

The statue's story
was commissioned by Mid Wales Arts

Just To Say, 2023
was published online by CultureMatters
and Yorkshire Bylines

Snapshot
was published in Indelible #6

15, Darlington St
was commissioned by Asylum Artist Quarter
as part of the 'if we had this space' project

and for those of you who enjoy poetry videos...
Fatima
and
15, Darlington St
can both be found on Youtube

This photo with friends

must have been taken in summer.
We are where paths meet in a park
looking unbelievably young
– fresh faced, taut skin, bouncing –
and we are laughing as we take it in turns
to push each other round in a shopping
trolley we've found somewhere and
wouldn't dream of thinking of returning.
Here is my first tattoo, here my anarcho-
crustie-mullet haircut, here the pair
of ragged combats I spent an afternoon
dyeing black and cut to just above the knee.
Here the flatness of my stomach, here
the espadrilles on my feet which will forever
smell of late lost nights and wet rope.
We are so young, all of us, so full of hope.
None of us have stumbled into dead-end
jobs or dead-end relationships, none of us
have woken to be told of a shadow on lung,
liver, bowel, the need to telescope plans
to the immediate, none of us are addicts yet,
and none of us have died. The sun
is shining. We have a shopping trolley.
I can hear us laughing even now.

Love song

there is this town –
not one you'll know, trust me on that.
it's not the site of a famous battle
or on the list of *50 places you must go!!*
it isn't the jumping-off point for a hike
in snow-capped mountains
it isn't a hasn't-been-discovered-by-the-masses-yet
wonder of a hangout that only you and your friends know

this town doesn't make a bean from the tourist dollar
or the daily disgorging of coach parties falling over
themselves to get the perfect picture on insta or FB
this town isn't the destination of stag parties or hen-dos,
no-one comes here for romantic breaks or a long weekend
when the need to get away from the kids/job/neigh-
bours/family/delete as appropriate
simply overwhelms

it has no sea view, you'll find no sunsets
over ocean or hills,
no cathedral, no stately home
it hasn't got a pier, the canal wharves are all gone
there are no charming little bistros
tucked up back streets booked up weeks in advance
with simple starters from under a tenner!!
the king does not have one of his many palaces here

premier league footballers
wouldn't touch this place with yours
it has no stadia, no concert halls
there is no rudimentary airport
which Ryanair has given the name of a city
fifty miles away at the other end of a two-hour bus ride
which smells of disappointment, exhaustion and
the inevitable unravelling of your relationship

(other budget airlines are available, they may be better,
it's a lucky dip)

this town has no sky-scrape, glass-front office blocks
the nearest thing it has to a financial hub
is when the dealers are busy in the car park
of an evening, getting by and getting high
it's not a *pied-a-terre* for money men from London
where they meet up with a mistress
have an afternoon 'off-grid'
no X marks the spot
there's no treasure buried

Gisele Buendchen and Naomi Campbell
have not been seen
scouring the charity shops for bargains
picking up second-hand copies

of Jordan's 4th autobiography for a song
it is not plagued by paparazzi
don't get me wrong
these are not complaints
it's just the way it is

there is this town
we live here

it's our secret.

The polski sklep has closed its doors

for the last time. And this morning
in the June heat, men are hauling
the awkward empty bulk of chiller units

from shop to pavement to truck,
already sweating. Cursing in a language
we claim we do not understand

but speak too well. A lexicon
of loss and hurt and pain,
the job that disappears

a ladder climbed that turns
to snake again. Small dreams stuffed
in plastic bags in overflowing bins.

On the other side of Market Square,
where the breeze cools, we stand
idle in shade, and watch.

The lad next to me is smiling,
confusing the hammer falling
– for once – elsewhere,

with something like a win.

A fat man celebrates his place
in the universe

Friday night, stumbling home
three sheets to the wind,
he orders a kebab
with all the trimmings

lets the hot fat of Ursa Major
run down his chin
leans back against the wall
watches the stars in wonder.

Wakes hungering for more.
Full english down the greasy spoon
chomps on charred sausages, fires onion
rings into the black hole of his mouth

spreads toast with butter flown in
from god knows where, gorges on
the soft exploding nebulae of fried eggs,
bacon the flavour of life on far-off worlds.

By evening, he is making a decaying orbit
of the high street, has battered down
the chippy door hunting for scraps,
wolfing molten cheese of a pizza supernova

gobbling through constellations laced with lard,
keeps one watchful eye on the Milky Way
turning slowly overhead, feels galaxies
glowing and churning inside him.

In praise of the hardiness of market traders

the lady with the market stall
      is there on Wednesdays,
            come shine come rain

all her goods set out on
      a hundred cardboard boxes
            come shine come rain

sheep's feet, dog chews, tripe-flavoured treats, seed
      for pigeons and parrots, robin and budgies
            come shine come rain

the last lass gave it up for a job in a building
      society, warmth of an office
            come shine come rain

for the promise of sick pay, holiday pay, steady
      hours, the security of wages
            come shine come rain

perhaps this one's made of sterner stuff, face lined and
      smiling, hands busy with fags and matches
            come shine come rain

I hope so, visit her each week for the banter
      and the laughter, buy pigs' ears for foxes
            come shine come rain

The library staff deal with another enquiry

Gary would like to know
the names of the twelve apostles.
He's here in the library
asking for a book about
the twelve apostles,
any book, a kids' one will do,
just a book with the names
of the twelve apostles
– Jesus's twelve apostles –
and what they did.
I mean, what did they do
for a living? Gary asks.
There was the one who was
a fisherman, right?
But the rest of them?
What did they do?
Is there a book on it?
He thought the library would
have a book, a book
on the twelve apostles,
their names, and what they
stood for. They must have stood
for something. Is there a book?
There should be a book.
Gary would like a book.

The sun is shining at last, and

as I work outside the black guy
with half a mouth of teeth and
a rasta belt holding up his
raggy jeans stops to say this
is a beautiful house, that he stood
as a kid in the queue along the street
to collect his mom's prescriptions,
asks after the old doctors, both of them,
shakes his head when I tell him they
are no longer with us, says the house
is beautiful, should stay beautiful,
stands tall in his workboots, waves
wearily at the world, tells me they're
erasing our history, tearing down what
we were, destroying our town.

I tell him we will look after the house.
Hope that we can. On the car park
a crow pecks greedily at a stolen egg
the wood pigeons still haven't realised is gone.

Sitting in his doorway on the High Street, Darren's thoughts are as slippery as eels

i.
Right now, he knows one thing,
that it couldn't be better. He can't
explain why – maybe it's the way the light
picks out the gold in the brickwork,
how it dances off the tarmac,
puts smiles on the faces of the people
walking by – maybe it's that. And
maybe it's something more.

ii.
Whatever, he knows one thing,
that it doesn't matter. He can't
explain why – he just slides
through the gaps in the brickwork,
bounces off night-time tarmac,
turns his eyes from the faces of the people
walking by – an itch to scratch. And
maybe a need to score.

iii.
Always, he knows one thing,
that home is in tatters. He can't
explain why – he just hides
his past behind brickwork,
stays silent as tarmac,
home is for others, those people
walking by – so fuck that. And
this is him. Here. In this door.

And this...

is for those politicians and journalists
who will now sing the praises
of life spent in public service

who are indifferent to nurses
at food banks, care not for civil servants
who cannot heat their homes

remain silent about pensioners
lying in their own piss
in corridors in A&E

who will never say they met
a dinner lady once, how she
was a wonderful wonderful woman

who never stood in the rain at the gates
to the crem, awaiting a coffin,
offering heartfelt condolences
to family and friends.

Crown & Sceptre, Friday 9th September, 4.15pm

and Niall is telling the barmaid he's going to ring the lawyer he
is he is he's going to ring the lawyer as she nods and smiles
nods and smiles and pours because it's doing his head in it's
doing his bastard head in and yeah go on he'd like another
Bud and he prowls like a tiger in a backwater pub where all
the screens are set to sports channels but there are
no sports to show

and Shane and Mark pop in for just a quick one to wash
the Junction 10 dust from the back of their throats and
the quick one will be four or five at least as Shane and Mark
and the barmaid all know and she smiles and pours and
smiles and smiles and pours and they've a regular wage
and hi-vis, you can see them both from space and all
the screens are set to horse racing
but there's no horse race

and the lads who drank at The Eagle until The Eagle
closed are at the table in the corner so they can see
who comes and goes the barmaid pours their lager
pours their lager pours their lager and they offer her
a grin and the sports channels say no football and
yes this means that this week you can't lose
it doesn't mean you ever win

and they're all bucket hats and swagger and they're ready
to take flight and one of them's a mouth that's guaranteed
to lead his fists into a fight and the barmaid keeps an eye
on them and they think she could be flirting but she's

smiling pouring nodding and she thinks she's almost certain
that laughter's not offensive kicking a ball is nothing wrong
and channels made for sport should have some sport on

and the men who last had jobs when there were factories
in this town who have a Friday evening pint as if the work
was still around and the plasterers and painters and the
plumbers and the drivers and the blokes who have a market
stall the shift workers and skivers are all in here for the *craic*
a pint perhaps who knows a short and the barmaid smiles and
nods and smiles and nods and smiles and nods and pours
in this backwater pub on a Friday where sports channels
don't show sport

Corodividednation

by now, of course, you'll know
the way the day panned out

mid-morning, the mood dark
as skies, heavy as policing

abbey filled with the great and good
whose mouths taste of leather

whose souls are spreadsheets
their world an unending transaction

who watch the robe presented
to a rough sleeper curled in a doorway

on Euston Road his filthy sleeping bag
laid upon the monarch's shoulders

the holy oil, brought up the aisle
in a dinghy found on Dover beach

to Canterbury, life-jacketed, sodden,
who drips salt water and the echo of prayers

in Albanian, Dari, Farsi, and homegrown
poverty over the heads of the congregation

the jewelled sword of offering
the bracelets of sincerity and wisdom

pawned for foodbanks in forgotten towns
where bread and tinned goods count for more

than any circus

that Black Power salute
a thing of wonder

nightingale singing in Berkeley Square
the Thames running out to the sea

On living with a larger, expansionist neighbour

you know he has always coveted
your garden, considered to be his
by right the olive trees, the earth,
that access to the sea, believes

your home an extension of his own,
tells himself that you are leading
him on, asking for trouble,
driving him crazy by smiling

too much, by not smiling enough,
by smiling at all, flaunting that
independence you're so proud of,
dressed in that provocative

geography he can't get out of
his mind, refusing his advances,
gardening your land without
so much as a by his leave

while he presses himself tight
up against your borders,
belly over the waistband of
his trousers, simmering to fury

planning for the morning you
will wake to find the front door
off its hinges, the olive trees
your grandparents planted

chopped and cut to kindling, his
tanks flattening your flowerbeds
and him blocking the way to your
kitchen, stripping the fridge bare,

not expecting you to fight.

Newport, Shropshire. 23rd March, 10.15am

Everything is bathed in pale Spring sunshine,
there is blue sky, soft white blossom on the trees
the air-raid sirens are not sounding their alarm
and the man in hi-vis in the middle of the road
spraying markings for a reason we do not know,
is just someone else not buried under rubble.
The Barley has its doors open for morning trade
and a woman in a mobility scooter, late
for an appointment, slaloms through
shoppers. We have not learned to
recognise the whistle of incoming shells,
delivery drivers are still smiling
a boy in a mask waits at the bus stop
ready to travel to who knows where

the library has not yet been bombed.

[here], plodding on

[here] outside the coffee shop
when I ask if I can help

[here] in the shopping centre
where to let signs sprout like weeds

she can't go in with her dog
passes me her dog
checks I won't run off with her dog

[here] men sit on benches the weight
of the world on their shoulders

faces turned in, shuttered,
vacant, uncertain, lost

[here] the clock on its tower
above us has no hands

and we have all the time
we need, or none at all

[here] I am cradling a stranger's dog
in watery sunshine, a cold wind

waiting
watching

[here] she comes, the dog
is pleased to see her

she says she used to keep
collies, but her legs

and the dog nestles under her coat
as she rolls to my table

we plod on, don't we?

[here] a girl has brought her vanilla
slice and milky coffee

and she is telling me
she met her husband in a disco

[here] it's never the looks – she taps her chest –
it's always, always in the heart

and the scooter is a godsend
but she's waiting for a car

[here] he topped himself last year
the daughter has learning difficulties, but

we plod on, don't we?

she's a good girl,
has part-time work

[here] they moved, of course, after
thirty-four years together, gone

we plod on, don't we?

[here] she doesn't see things getting better
believes they're getting worse, but

we plod on, don't we?

I finish my coffee, shake
her hand, say it's good

to have met her [here]
we plod on, don't we?

in the middle of some
unfolding slow disaster

the ground not yet settled
we plod on, don't we?

we plod on
[here]

still a way to fall.

Old man in The Scotia

has to be shown, three times
how to set the capo.

Can't find the right chords
the key which will unlock

the door to the tune
he knows he left here somewhere.

Searches the faces round him
for clues, memory, inspiration

wets his lips with *uisge*
offers a prayer up. Perseveres.

And now his fingers fall on frets
the way they used to

his soft voice rises, strengthens
into song. For these few minutes

the chemo doesn't matter
the dying doesn't matter

as conversation stills to silence
and the walls lean in to listen

and he sees faded angels dancing
on the heads of dropping pins.

On holiday in Scotland, Cassandra waits for daybreak

when I wake in the night
the summered hills to the north-east
threaten the first cinder glow of dawn
the river is burning mercury and gold
is liquid fire, a mirrored sky I could
step into, fall down down down forever

further south, the land bakes
watercourses run dry
the weak die, men hide away indoors
here, mist ebbs and flows
on grassland like tides
tendrils of smoke drift on water

oystercatcher shriek alarms
about the day to come
in the twilit shallows heron strike
jubilantly at small fish
I sleep fitfully, and all of us wait

the sun will burst upon us soon enough

For George

under a darkening sky
we sit round a log fire
out there cities are burning
the planet is burning and

i can't breathe

out there people are dying
in hospitals in care homes
alone in bedsits   with the knee
of a cop pressed into their neck and

i can't breathe

out there pepper spray   nightstick
rubber bullet   rage
the same wrongs the old injustice
complicity complacency and

i can't breathe

in the darkness we search
for each other   for hope
for the glimmerings of dawn
for words   but what words are there
we haven't used before?

listen   fucking listen

i can't breathe
i can't breathe
i can't breathe

This should be simple

(a poem for UN anti-racism day)

This should be simple.

No-one is born racist.
No child is born hating another child
for their language, their food, or their name.
A road which leads to ethnic cleansing,
pogroms, rivers of blood
is not mapped
is a road that is laid
step by step, stone by stone
can be undone step by step
stone by stone.

This should be simple.

No system has to be racist.
A pattern of institutionalised inequality
where you're more likely to be excluded from school
more likely to end up in jail
more likely to die prematurely
more likely to find that you fail
can be unpicked stitch by stitch
law by law, day by day
must be unpicked law by law,
day by day.

This should be simple.

We all breathe the same air
drink the same water
share the same dreams for our children
and hopes for our future.

You cannot show me the melanin in laughter
the ethnicity of a smile
we all rise or fall together
do as you would be done by
we all rise or fall together.

This should be simple.

7.19 in the evening, and the boy outside

New Street station is singing
a lament for us all, he sings

for the puffa jacket kids clothed
and camouflaged in swagger, he sings

for the electric bike takeaway riders
who criss-cross the city, silent

and determined, their two-wheel
spinning gig economy, he sings

for the husk of a lad who totters
tram tracks like a ballerina, trailing

a sleeping bag, who is going nowhere
good in his own slow time and is lost

to us, he sings
for the young couples, still

in love, touching hands
and clasping ready meals

heading back to city apartments
to share each other's dreams, he sings

for football fans and figures folded
in the shadow of doorways, he sings

for shift workers, their aching backs
their fallen arches, he sings

for the quiet conversation of women
on their way to clean offices, he sings

for the is this isn't this
flirtation of friends, he sings

for our mistakes, our wrong turnings
our missed opportunities, the bright future

that slipped through our fingers, the better
world that disappeared, he sings

and his voice, pure and soft, a gift
spirals out to join satellites and stars

seeking nothing but the joy of its own being
an offering to god, if god is listening

and I think, we should all be crying
here, we should all of us be crying

it is 7.19 in the evening and
the boy outside New Street station sings

Your slow vibration

"…life is only a dream, and we are the imagination of ourselves."
Bill Hicks

somewhere you are sailing
up the St Lawrence seaway still,
into a new found land, an opening future

the job you will walk out of
is still waiting, while in a dusty depot
on the edge of town a tired man
in stained overalls and a lifetime's pain
is counting down the hours till sleep
and week's end, filling diesel tanks on locos
which will one day barrel you west west west
through mountain range to ocean

you have not yet boomeranged back
by bus from shining sea to sea
not taken your seat on a jet plane
where the nervous stewardess
is practising her welcome smile
hoping the new uniform suits her
you've not watched Idlewild slip away
you've still to taste a drink at eight miles high

the woman you will wed
is right now still unmarried
lives in digs in a city far away from home
and whether the years will leave her childless
or she'll hold your new-born

in her arms, one after another
after another after another
is still unknown

you have not written yourself
into this town, these streets,
not woven yourself into our lives
and that day has not yet come
when I will touch my fingers
to your cold, still hand
whisper my good bye,
and tell myself that somewhere

you are sailing, wind in your face,
up the St Lawrence seaway still,
into your new found land,
and some opening, glittering future.

A son writes...

Well, you can imagine the scale of the job.
A place this size, all those rooms, and nooks
and crannies. Eighty years of clutter and him
never throwing anything away. There's tins
in the pantry from when you were still with us,
and your writing on the wipe-clean board
cocoa, whole almonds, dried onion, eggs
as if you've popped out down the shops
and will be back any minute. In other news,
the trees have gone. No, not all of them.
The two at the back, felled. The house is filled
with light, and I've wood to last three winters.
No. I haven't been to mass in years, but can
rattle off a Hail Mary like I learned it yesterday.
These things run deep. I hope that makes you
smile. He'll have told you himself now,
there wasn't a day he didn't miss you.
I know I never visit. My one regret is this:
I shouldn't have listened to my sister.
I should have thumped that fucking priest.

In a moment's pause on night shift, a British nurse considers the nature of the strong message she must send to Mr Putin

This letter comes to you, President
Putin, from another, better world. Here,
Nadhim is once again working the graveyard
shift – hospital basement, concrete tunnels,
the flick flick flickering striplight no-one cares
to fix, his muscles aching, the bus ride back
to a cold flat on the wrong side of town still
hours away, the sealed bags of surgical waste
he must toss into the furnace that little bit
too heavy for a man as old as he, his pay
packet always that little bit too small, while
the   one   slow   clap   that   plays
on repeat on his headphones does nothing
to help Nadhim put food on the table, meet his bills.

And you, Vladimir?
Oh, you won't even exist.
This letter will never need to be.

Me? I will be as busy as ever.
Today we open Nadhim's former home
to refugees, will offer the young couple
from Palestine room for the night
in the comfort and warmth
of his legendary stables,
will wait for miracles.

El Vaquita

I've always been my own master.
Howl at the moon if the fancy takes me, yes,
– who wouldn't? – but mostly all I ask
is a full belly, sunshine,
a stroll round the harbour
with a weather eye on the *pescadores*,
a nose in the arse of old friends,
then *siesta* in the afternoon.
Sniff at lampposts, scratch for fleas,
enjoy the quiet life. That's me.

I answer to no man.
But when the marching starts,
my ears prick, I slide like water
down alleyways, *calle*, slip
between legs, beneath patting hands
to the front line.

I have a nose for injustice,
teeth for what is wrong.
On our own, we are nothing.
Together, strong.
I've felt the boot of the oppressor
in my ribs before. Not having it.
No mas! No mas! No mas! No more.

A thousand curses on the bastard *policia* who shoots me.
May he never lick his own balls again
or scent a bitch in heat.

May his mother's spaniel piss in his jackboots,
smear his silken handkerchiefs with shit.

Xmas is a quiet doorway in the shade,
a dull throb, licking my wounds. But,
when my people march again,
I join them. We are the pack.
Whoever we are fighting for this time,
venceremos! No turning back.

Viva El Vaquita!
Viva… me?
Mother of God, may I be born again
a dog with two dicks.
This is solidarity, people
of my *barrio*, this is

you, *veterinario* with the kind eyes,
hands that are gentle. I won't run.
Do what you must. I trust you.
Heal me quickly – there is fighting to be done.

Heal me quickly – there is fighting to be done

let us rise, all of us, from our sickbeds
spring from the back of ambulances
paramedics trailing behind us
let us leave our wards, fill the outside world
in our hordes, in hospital gowns
that cannot help but show
our arse to all who care to look
as well as those who don't
let us wheel ourselves, carrying
each other's drips, limping on crutches,
testing out our artificial hips
let our pacemaker-governed hearts set
the beat as we march through traffic,
along pavements, down streets, over bridges,
with our butterfly-stitched knife wounds
the gaps where should be missing limbs
and the bloody unwanted medals of industrial injuries
let us shuffle in our bandages
with our swollen ankles, our weeping sores
our asthma inhalers, our cornucopia of pills
let us rise, every last one of us,
battered, scarred, broken, frail,
beautiful and enduring,
let us rise

Fatima

Fatima's working in cyber
she's learned how to snoop and to hack
she's talented, driven, and passionate
her revenge a cold feast, not a snack

Rishi's bank account there on a spreadsheet
a few clicks of the keys, and... goodbye
Hancock's now being sought on charges of fraud
Gove for intent to supply

Cummings just never existed
his records amended, deleted
Johnson pursued for child maintenance payments
left penniless, bankrupt, defeated

Rees-Mogg's found his place in a workhouse
learning to do what he's told
and a freighter inches towards St Helena
with Priti Patel in the hold

Yes, Fatima's working in cyber
she's smart, and she seizes her chances
at the end of the day, puts her laptop away

picks her shoes up

                    and smiles as she dances.

The statue's story

I am born of dragons
of furnace and imagination
fractured, broken fragments
made a greater sum
under low cloud or blue cathedral
the seasons and their cycle
blessed by rain and soft light
frost and summer sun

I am the child of alchemy
of fire and of toil,
rejoicing in kite's circling and raven call
rivers that run to the sea
wind blowing in from ocean
see me lean into the caress
of spring storms, gales of autumn

and when you put your ear
to my clay-caked lips

let me whisper
secret prayers of miners
in the dropping, rattling cage
laughter of shop-girls
piety of chapel and righteous rage
hum lullabies of lost, drowned villages of Elan
soft, easy promises of publicans
and salesmen
let me raise our history
treasure after muttered treasure

ghosts of neighbours and the sacrament
of gossip, passed on
on doorsteps and street corners
Bread of Heaven and backstreet brawlers
drunken Friday nights
the wild dreams of farmers
wrapped tight in sweat-soaked sheets,
hearts racing across hillsides

and know that
last night I listened again
to the singing of train tracks,
heard echoes from the north and west
ringing down the steel
It made me feel… restless, defiant

tomorrow we will force open the gates,
my tribe and I,
march west under moonlight
guided by the certainty of memory and stars,
hitch the last few miles to the coast at dawn
in the cab with a delivery driver chasing the morning
half-crazed by lack of sleep and opportunity

I promise you we shall
wash ourselves clean in cold salt water
lay our heads down in caverns
deep beneath mountains
curl ourselves round a familiar eternity
and wait

How simple the art of re-ravelling

A homeless man wakes in a doorway
unflattens cardboard into boxes sits
with his dog throwing coins from
a paper cup to random strangers
hands a sandwich to a woman on
her lunch break a coffee to a pensioner
in need one week later he is clean
and shaven his sleeping bag is new
tomorrow he will walk back to a
waiting flat where a landlord will
help him carry furniture carpet TV
up the stairs reduce his rent offer him
an envelope of money on the first
of each and every month. Next day
he wakes, dresses. Goes to his new job,
is greeted by friends.

The city's journey

starts
with a clearing
a scraping of fields, turnips, beans
a straggle of huts downhill
to the stream
every part of a pig but the squeal

splashes
through the ford
to the press of crowds at the market
milk, butter, cloth
acrobats and jugglers
butchers and the stink of blood

slips
into the alehouse for a quick one
stays longer than it should
like always
comes out as dark falls
a maze of alleyways and passages
proper houses, built of wood

stumbles
past plague pits
hangings, priests, and executions
mailed fists of sheriff's men
some bigshot building a castle

then war war war
and for a century or more
can't move for farriers, blacksmiths
swordsmiths, fletchers
women and their soldiers

and – out of nowhere – peace

strides
into the guildhall
spouting plans, negotiations, deals
embracing trade and strangers
printing press, coffee, the potato
one invention after the other
profit upon profit, bags of gold

shimmies
into gaslight
the miracle of sewers
sidings, canals, and locomotion
the municipal park
courting under the belch of the furnace
engineers with instruments and pens

sprawls
into concrete, visions, motorways
building for the sky
suburbs, the commute, and aspirations
a world of neon and endless plenty

stutters
choking on gridlock,
austerity, the tightening of belts
retreating to patch, make do, and mend

squats
before a million flickering computers
sighs and dreams
screensaver of a clearing
a scraping of fields
the straggle of huts downhill
to a stream.

Just To Say, 2023:
an oil executive holds forth

(after William Carlos Williams)

I have eaten
the future
that was in
the pipeline

and which
you were probably
saving
for your children

Forgive me
it was delicious
so profitable
and so cold

For the drivers stuck in three miles of stationary traffic, M6 southbound, junctions 10A to 10

you who are trying to deliver a van load
of pallets to somewhere near Slough,
who are late for work at the new job
in admin in the centre of Birmingham,
who have been sent to Coventry, again,
you who are regretting that third cup
of coffee when the morning was still young
you who meant to set out ten minutes earlier
but hit snooze on the alarm, twice
you who are kicking yourselves to no good end
you who are lost
you who are grieving
you whose bladder is full to bursting
with no services in view,
you who have been away from home
for weeks and cannot walk through
the front door a moment too soon
you who have been staring at the back
of a Lithuanian truck since what feels like
shortly before the dawn of time, who are wondering
what life is like there, whether the driver too is cursing
these three slow miles, and how,
you who are resolving to learn to curse
the Highways Agency fluently, inventively
in Lithuanian, Hungarian, Greek,
in every language of the world
you who are bored
you who are restless
you who are using this time to re-evaluate

your life choices and finding them
largely unsatisfactory
you who are lonely
you who are dreaming of lovers
you who wish you'd caught the train
you who are using every trick in the book
to entertain five-year-olds
but exhausted the possibilities of I-spy
two hundred yards and an hour or more ago,
you who are watching the fuel gauge drop to empty
with a sense of despair
you who are singing along to your favourite
music at the top of your voice
without a care in the world
you who are in a murderous rage
you who are managing calls on the hands-free
who have vital documents stuck in the boot
who cannot afford to lose this contract
cannot afford to lose this contract
you who are cutting in to get one place
forward in the queue not giving a tuppenny
toss that everyone hates you
you who are at the end of your tether
who are beyond the end of your tether
who have given up entirely
on tethers

all of you, as you pass over
the gold ribbon of the old canal
caught in your slow crawl

see how the heron opens his great wings,
glides, reflected in the water,

                    and lands.

Kevin the commuter casts off the chains

Friday night train out of the city.
Jammed in the cheek to jowl to blank stare
bray of others on the phone
Kevin can almost taste the coming freedom.

Pops into the shop by the station.
Treats himself to a meal for one
a bottle of *blanc*. And another.
Whistles his way home.

Key in the door. Jacket on the hook.
Briefcase flung down on the floor.
Meal ready for the microwave.
Tie loosened. Glass poured.

Stairs taken two at a time.
Shirt, trousers, work shoes flung
somewhere near the laundry basket.
Over there.

Music on.
Shaves before the mirror
humming along to *My Way*.
Shower as hot as it's possible to bear.

Wrapped in the caress of a bathrobe
and the pleasure of another glass of wine
thoughts turn to *Wonder what to wear?*
Hunts through drawers, joy rising.

Time for the soft sheer of hold-ups
the sweet silk of satin
the thigh-slit chinese dress
that slips and slides and clings.

Christina looks at herself in the mirror
pouts, applies the pillar-box red
adds lashes, mascara.
Honey, she's home. Her heart sings.

A superhero speaks

I'm not like those other charlatans
the new messiahs on Youtube or TV

all designer suits, capped smiles
calfskin boots and perfect hair

there to stare into the camera, eyes
aglow on adulation, tell how they raised

the dead, saved the passengers who bled out
in a bus crash, healed the victims of a bomb

theirs a humble story, an ordinary person
doing god's work, donations welcome

subscribe via the link, after dinner
speaking fees reasonable to astronomical

additional expenses as required
parking for private jet non-negotiable

no   that is not my way
that is not how I do this

but the man at the bus stop
with arthritic fingers

the friend in the cafe
with scarring on their lungs

I pat on the shoulder as I pass
offer a handshake or a hug

later that evening, or next day
they find they can hold a mug

without pain, climb stairs
without gasping

I choose to walk in a world
of small everyday miracles, see you

push that supermarket trolley
lay my hand on your shoulder

know that maybe you will, too

Snapshot

right now

she is dancing in her orange kitchen
like she hasn't a care in the world
see how she freestyles sunshine
is spinning rainbows   tiptoes barefoot gold
smiles as she dances, like no-one is watching

right now

she is cranking it up loud   louder   loudest
is singing along, makes up the words
she doesn't know, plays air guitar
like a virtuoso, holds the note.... waits....
swoops whoops stomps stomps stomps
when the beat drops in, dark and phat and dirty

right now

she's a spliff clasped in one hand
cider in the other
empty bottle on the worktop
four cooling, waiting in the fridge
silver jewellery catching the light
as sun pours in through evening window

right now

if you could paint a picture of perfection
of contentment, full and sated, a woman
at ease with herself and the world
you might choose to pick up your brush
capture this

right now

she can believe the days
when she is stretched so thin
when we are stretched so thin
when her head is visited by old ghosts
and cross-hatch scars itch beneath her sleeves
those days are gone forever

right now

she's turned away from everything
melting icecaps, forests burning
shut down the laptop, switched off the news
silenced the trolls and those who choose
to see tearing others down as some kind of validation
knock yourselves out – her life is, will be, a celebration

right now

she can breathe
she can dance
she can dream

right now

there is this moment
there is nothing but this moment

she is dancing in her orange kitchen
smiling as she dances,

                    and this is love

15, Darlington St

when we finally get the keys to our kingdom
– and it will be no easy thing, my brothers, my sisters,
my friends, no quick and easy thing, this will be a story
in itself –
when we finally get the keys to our kingdom
turn them in stiff and rusted locks
tumblers and pins re-learning old lessons
falling into place just as they always did

when we force open the doors
to stale air, the smell of dust, damp, abandonment
fast food flyers faded in heaps on the floor
bleached by the passing of the seasons
when we force open the doors
stand in our space, filling it with noise
rattling nineteen to the dozen
about what we will do with this blank canvas
plans spilling out of our open mouths
like diamonds

when we set to work
with mop and bucket and dustpan and brush
sweeping away mouse droppings, cobwebs
busy with plaster and fresh paint
when we set to work
so the history of this place can breathe again
the smudges of art in the corner of our vision
the joy of sight slipping sharply into focus
dresses that slide on like second satin skin
for past generations

when we throw open the windows
to let the world in
the morning sunshine which fills the first-floor room
copper gold on fresh-stripped floorboards
when we throw open the windows
let our music – african, latin, classical, dub,
rock, folk, disco, hard house, techno –
tumble to toe-tapping bus queues outside
where post office shoppers are smiling

when we cloak the building
in scaffolding, splendour it in something
about dancing and revolutions in letters nine feet high
reveal every square inch a colourful mural
when we cloak the building
in honeysuckle, jasmine, mile-a-minute
window boxes of lavender on every sill
clematis that covers the rooftops
create an oasis revealed in the heart of our city

when we fill this place
with laughter, and chat, the din of conversation
over coffee and cake, butter melting on fresh baked bread
soup ladled from the vat which steams
on the stove along the wall
when we fill this place
with full bellies – full bellies –
when hunger is no more
when we are sated together
united in hope, love, compassion

when out of darkness comes light
and on the roof garden up from the alley
in the moments after the rain stops
and the planet smells reborn anew
you lie on your back, stare into infinity,
the glory of a clear blue sky
know that out of darkness comes light
that anything is possible
that the miracle of bee-buzz and birdsong
was always there, waiting

when night falls, we will watch for shooting stars

Dumfries insurrection

On Glencaple quayside with the river flooding in,
the couple in the caravan strike up conversation
as curlew call around us, oystercatchers cry
and swallows hunt for insects late into the dusk.
We watch the wonder of the tidal bore, discuss
what you hear and see and learn to love
travelling in a horse-drawn bow-top
at twelve miles an hour, nothing above.
We talk about the things that are right
things that are wrong and always have been
about slipping away from it all and living in
the   beautiful   gaps   between
and in the laughter, camaraderie, and chat
she says, out of nowhere,

I'm waiting for the revolution.

Aren't we all, I tell her.
We're all waiting for that.

Early this morning

with the frost still thick
on the rooftops and the garden
plants curled in upon themselves
and the sun still not yet
over the horizon and the sky
the palest blue a hint of lemon
yellow in the south and east
and the din of the bin truck
rolling beeping slowly up
the street tipping recycling
into the maw that gapes open
and shuts and opens again
and I am outside in this
a crisp January morning
leaning on my crutch
standing on my one good
leg scattering grain
feeding pigeons who
come now when I call
and the morning is still
young and my breath is
soft clouds hanging in the air
and we are bright-eyed
all of us fearless all of us
and any moment
now that sun
will rise

If you want more poems, blogs,
and news of what I'm up to,
pop along to the website:

stevepottinger.co.uk

notes on some of the poems in this book

Love song: for forgotten towns, and the people in them.

A fat man celebrates: In 2018, scientists determined that space is full of grease and soot.

Crown & Sceptre: I popped into my local one afternoon, and all the sports channels were tuned in to a frenzy of national mourning. Madness.

Corodividednation: a re-imagining of all that ridiculous pomp and nonsense.

[here], plodding on: sometimes I'm lucky enough to meet the most remarkable people. This lady was one.

For George: George Floyd was murdered by a Minneapolis policeman who knelt on his neck for nine minutes. It's the 21st c. Time to put racism and police brutality to bed.

7.19 in the evening: this poem just unfolded in front of me.

In a moment's pause: in December 2022, nurses threatened to strike over pay. Conservative Chair Nadhim Zahawi urged them not to do so, saying that accepting a real terms pay cut would 'send a strong message' to the Russian leader. Yeah, right. Try this message, Nadhim.

El Vaquita: In 2020, a street dog in the city of Antofagasta in Chile was voted 'character of the year' in a popular poll in the local newspaper. El Vaquita was always present at demonstrations in the city, and was shot and wounded by a policeman while at a demo in late 2019. Unable to find him so he could be treated, the people of the city organized a fake demonstration. El Vaquita limped out of hiding, the demo made its way to a vets, and he was treated and restored to health. A lesson for us all, I feel.

Fatima: remember that government poster? *Fatima's next job could be in cyber – she just doesn't know it yet.* Be careful what you wish for…

The statue's story: Mid Wales Arts asked six poets to each write a piece about sculptures exhibited at the centre. My poem is a response to a statue by artist Alison Lochhead. There's a beautifully shot video of all six poets reading their pieces (mine's the final one) and you can watch them here https://midwalesarts.org.uk/videos/six-of-the-best

Snapshot: we need to celebrate these moments of joy more than ever. We really do.

15, Darlington St: a poem about one of the many empty buildings in Wolverhampton city centre. As part of Offsite BAS9, I was one of ten poets commissioned to write a poem imagining how we could bring some of those buildings back to life.

Dumfries insurrection: a true story.

Is there a bonus poem?

Of course there's a bonus poem.
Just turn the page.

It is 1983

or maybe 4, and we
are at Glastonbury
young, carefree, bathed
in sunshine and hope, and
I cannot remember where
it is we have been –
the green field, perhaps, or
the circus tent, or
to see the man who sells
trips from the back of his
van – but I am
with you, and you are ankle
bracelets, kohl, confidence,
a nest of backcombed hair
thick with festival dust
and two whole cans
of Harmony extra hold,
and you are dressed in what
may once have been a white
flowing dress, but isn't
three days in, you are cackling
laughter and sad smiling eyes
and we are on our way back
from wherever we have been,
weaving our way through
the crowd stretched out on grass
before the main stage, when
a band we've never seen
or heard of strike up and we
are transported, we are stopped

stand watch wonder eat
guitars, taste the trumpets
let the words tattoo themselves
softly on our skin, could stay here
in these moments for always, for
we have seen the big music
and we know we will
never be the same

and aren't, ever.

Ignite Books is a small, independent publisher. This book is the latest in our series which we hope puts thought-provoking, entertaining writing before a new audience. We have a lot of fun doing this, but we also survive on a shoestring budget and a lot of graft. So, if you've enjoyed this book, please tell your friends about us. You can also find us on Twitter*, so drop by and say hallo. And to learn more about what we do, or to shop for our other publications, you'll find our website at **ignitebooks.co.uk**

Thank you.

*It'll always be Twitter, Elon. Always.